The Lady's Season

A NOVELLA

Anne R Bailey

INKBL✦T PRESS

For my family

ALSO BY ANNE R BAILEY

Ladies of the Golden Age

Countess of Intrigue

The Pirate Lord's Wife

The Lady of Fortune

Forgotten Women of History

Joan

Fortuna's Queen

Thyra

Royal Court Series

The Lady Carey

The Lady's Crown

The Lady's Ambition

The Lady's Gamble

The Lady's Defiance

Bluehaven Series

The Widowed Bride

Choosing Him

Other

The Stars Above

You can also follow the author at: www.inkblotpressco.ca

CHAPTER 1

1602

There's nothing like these simple pleasures to put a smile on my face. The air around us is filled with the scent of burning pine. A servant places an ewer of spiced wine on the table between us. The fine fur of my borrowed robe tickles my throat as I pull it tight around me while my bare feet press into the plush carpet. I feel as content as an old cat languishing in front of a warm fire.

Across from me sits Bess, a faraway look in her eyes as she stares at the flickering flames. I know she is thinking of her husband, Sir Walter Raleigh, far from home. Queen Elizabeth named him governor of Jersey and tasked him with fortifying its defences. He'd promised to be home to celebrate the New Year, but alas, we haven't heard from him.

His work often keeps him away from Bess for years at a time. She knew this when she married him, yet it doesn't stop her yearning for him. It would be cruel to remind her it's better he's on a lonely island in the middle of the English Channel than here at home. The political climate is tense and Queen Elizabeth is Sir Walter Raleigh's only protector. Unfortunately for him, her impeccable health is failing. What will he do when she is gone? Across the border, King James of Scotland waits patiently for news of her death. He is likely to become our new monarch, and he hates Raleigh.

As I dwell on this, my own memories creep up on me. How many years have passed since the queen had my husband beheaded? It feels like an eternity, though it's only been two years. Every day stretched out longer than the last, as I struggled to keep my family clothed and fed. The shadow of poverty is still hanging over me. I may rely on the charity of my kind friends, but at least I no longer fear for my children. I have placed them around the country in the household of noble gentlemen to be educated as befits their station. In time, perhaps, my son will even have his earldom restored to him.

I force myself to take a breath and try to distract myself from the growing panic lodging itself in my throat. Reaching for the ewer, I fill both our cups with the steaming liquid and take a delicate sip.

Bess, sensing the shift in my mood, rests a hand on my arm. "What is it, Frances?"

"I am haunted by old memories and worry about what further troubles life holds for me," I say, hating the bitterness in my tone. I had meant to make a joke.

Her hand squeezes in a comforting gesture. "Well,

focus on the next few days instead. The house will be full of friends and we shall celebrate every day."

"I look forward to it," I say, rushing to reassure her. "I am grateful you invited me."

She hums in agreement. I catch the mischievous smile on her lips before she hides it by taking a drink from her cup.

Suspicion fills me. "Bess, what are you planning?"

"Nothing," she says, waving me away. "I'm glad to give you the opportunity to take your mind off your troubles. You never know what will happen."

I frown. "Why do I get the feeling I should flee?"

"After all I've done for you," Bess says, scolding me. "You have a duty to stay by my side, no matter what. Especially since Walter is clearly intent on abandoning me for another Christmas season."

"Exactly. Can you blame me for being concerned? Who knows how you plan to take advantage of this opportunity to torment me?"

Bess chuckles, twirling the end of her long braid around her fingers. "Nothing terrible. But I do think it's high time you cease this self-imposed exile. You are still young. You cannot go on living life like a nun."

I choke on some wine. "Bess, my experience with marriage has differed greatly from your own passionate affair."

"Who said anything about marriage?" she asks, with a wicked smile.

We both laugh but I suspect for two very different reasons.

"Trust me." Her eyes are wide and sincere.

I swallow back my doubts. I do trust her. A small part of me even agrees with her. I have to find joy in life again otherwise, I shall be doomed to nothing but misery and bitter memories.

～

Having helped Bess finalise her plans for the coming weeks, I am beside her as she greets the first arrivals. I help see that they are comfortable and want for nothing. Truth be told, I keep looking for excuses to keep myself away from the great chamber where everyone has gathered. Bess, noticing my absence, finds me lurking in one of the long galleries, absentmindedly looking out a window at the falling snow outside.

"Frances, you must join us," she says, using the same tone she uses on her son.

"I shall." I promise her.

Once she has retreated back to her guests and the noise of the hall, I steel myself. Then have to laugh at how ridiculous I am being. Haven't I faced worse? When the cannons were rolling up to my Essex estate I did not flinch. Why am I hesitating now?

I slip into the room without great fanfare. Glancing around, I am pleased by how it's all come together. Musicians play from a hidden alcove. All that is left is the garlands of pine, ivy and holly to be strung around the house. In keeping with tradition, Bess' growing collection is tucked away in storage awaiting Christmas eve. We should all be pious and grave leading up to the holiday season. As I look around at the cheerful faces, I know the priest would disapprove. I note many familiar faces. These were people I used to consider my friends. Of course, that was before my husband's rebellion against the queen. Some give me a nod in greeting, but others subtly turn their backs away from me. I can't blame them. Not really. But it makes me appreciate friends like Bess, who stood by me even more.

I make my way over to her, and she smiles warmly when she sees me.

"Lady Frances, so happy you could join us," she says with a smile. Those around her make a point of greeting me politely.

"You will excuse me, ladies," Bess says with a smile. "I must take my guest of honour to be introduced to everyone."

She pulls me away, and before I know it, I am whisked away once more. I've lost count of the number of times I say, "it's a pleasure to meet you." Bess has invited the usual crowd, but she's also expanded her social circle to include several unmarried gentlemen. I wouldn't have been suspicious if she hadn't hinted about her intentions.

"And here at last is Lord Richard Burke, Earl of Clanricarde," Bess says.

I pull back even as Bess draws me forward. He turns to face me and I draw in a deep breath to steady myself. The last time I saw him, he was urging me to take his horse to flee the queen's army. It was because of him that my children and I escaped before the cannons bombarded my home. But Bess couldn't know that. I never spoke about that terrible day to anyone. Is that why my heart is pounding wildly in my chest? Am I fearful of the memories seeing him will reignite?

My mind finally stops churning when we are face to face. He regards me warmly. There's no reproach or pity in his eyes. I would've fled if there was.

"I've longed to be officially introduced to you, Lady Frances," he says, bowing before kissing the back of my hand.

My cheeks heat at his words. I'm at a loss for words as he pulls away to stand a polite distance away.

Bess looks between the two of us, her mischievous grin unmistakable as she excuses herself. I want to call out to her, say something to make her stay, but it's too late.

Courtly manners kick in and I turn to him.

"I hope your journey here was pleasant. Were the roads good?" I ask, desperately wishing I had some wine to cool my nerves.

"Yes, I came up from London."

"Are you often in England? I thought you would be needed to manage your grand estates in Ireland."

Humour fills his pale blue eyes. "That sounds like a rebuke. Or perhaps you wish I was in Ireland?"

He has a way of speaking that leaves me confused. Is he being serious or just teasing? One thing is certain — I'm out of practice. "Please accept my sincere apology. I did not mean to reproach you."

His chuckle is low. "Lady Frances, I was merely teasing. I don't have a talent for conversation. You are right, I should be caring for my lands but the queen has summoned me and thus, you find me here in England." His face contours into a rueful expression. "When my father was on his deathbed he made me promise I would look after our people. I wonder if he'd approve of me. I feel torn in half by my responsibilities. Though my problems are nothing compared to others."

If it wasn't for his disarming charm and openness, his familiarity would've put me off. Desiring to comfort him, my hand reaches out to touch his forearm, but I stop myself at the last moment. "Don't disparage yourself. Not on my account." Words keep alluding me, so I decide now is as good as any time to thank him. "I never got the chance to let you know how grateful I am for the assistance you gave me in Essex all those years ago."

He's watching me silently. Is he waiting for more?

Clearing my throat, I say, "I know you must have others you wish to speak to. I appreciate you giving me the chance to thank you."

It's the wrong thing to say. I know it is even before I watch him retreat behind a mask of cool indifference. I'm about to say something else when he gives me a curt nod, cutting me off from any further platitudes.

"I understand, Lady Frances. I won't keep you any longer," he says, and I feel my throat tighten. Does he think my words are meaningless? The truth is so far from it.

"Lord Richard, no one wishes to associate with me. Not after —" I pause, taking a breath. "I have been in self-imposed exile for since the Earl of Essex's death." He notes how I cannot bring myself to call him my husband.

"Please understand how indebted and grateful to you I feel. Who knows what would've become of us had you not helped me. Others may put up with me for Lady Bess' sake, but you — you honour me. So please don't think I'm tongue tied in your presence because I wish to escape your company. I'm merely surprised to find you would want to speak to me."

He is taken aback by my honest candour. "There's no need to thank me. There was nothing heroic about me helping you. But that is in the past and we gain nothing by dwelling on it." His good humour returns. "I'm relieved to discover you don't wish to avoid my company."

"We can congratulate ourselves on narrowly avoiding a comical misunderstanding." I give him a weary smile.

He nods. "At least our story won't lead to any tragic conclusion."

"Are you implying we have some sort of future together?" I ask.

He grins and doesn't argue. As a widow twice-over, I cannot help but say, "in my experience, tragedy is waiting just around the corner."

Lord Richard, who knows of my history, is still confident when he says, "your prejudice is getting the better of you. Do not let your past dictate your future. Nor are we some characters in a play. We are two reasonable adults, unhindered by family and free to do as we choose." He looks over his shoulder before turning back to me. "And now I'd love to have you dance with me. Will you do me the honour?"

I agree and just like that, I'm swept into a lively country dance.

If anyone is shocked that the earl is dancing with the disgraced widow of a traitor, I don't notice. My eyes are fixed on him and the smile tugging at the corner of his lips. The sound of music and laughter silences any doubts. Soon I'm joining in too. When Richard lifts me high into the air and spins me round, I let out a squeal of delight.

As the dance comes to an end, I'm grinning from ear to ear. Richard whispers, "I hope I shall have the pleasure of dancing with you again soon."

Breathless, I can only nod.

We part for the sake of decorum, but throughout the evening, I find myself searching for him in the crowd. Once he catches me watching him. Our eyes lock and neither of us can look away.

The door to the bedchamber swings open with a crash. I shoot up in the bed with a scream already half-formed on my lips. Bess, who'd been sleeping beside me, has fallen out of bed in her haste to get to her feet.

My heart is pounding as I take in the dark shape standing in the doorway. Where are the guards?

"Peace," he says, stepping forward. "Is this to be my welcome?"

My mind is still groggy from being awoken so abruptly, so I struggle to place the familiar voice. Bess has less trouble.

"Good God, Walter, is that you?" She says, placing a hand over her heart.

He holds up the lit taper to illuminate his face. I slip out of bed with as much dignity as I can muster. He is grinning, clearly pleased with the effect his dramatic entrance has had on us.

"I promised you I would come and here I am," he says. His lips form a pout as he regards his wife. "I had hoped for a warmer welcome."

Bess runs forward and embraces him, kissing his cheeks, and lips before pushing him away. "You, dog. Scaring me like that. I thought I was about to be murdered as I slept."

Incorrigible as ever, Walter Raleigh tosses his head back and laughs. "Bad roads and foul weather slowed me down. I could've arrived with great fanfare in the morning, but I felt — no — I needed to see you without delay."

"Oh, Walter," Bess leans her head against his chest as he embraces her. "I was beginning to lose hope."

The scene is becoming too intimate.

"Please excuse me," I say, before slipping out of the room.

The presence chamber outside is quiet and cold. My heart is still pounding wildly in my chest as I glance at the Italian clock on the desk. It's just after five in the morning. I doubt I will be able to fall back asleep even though the sky outside remains dark and impenetrable.

Rather than wander aimlessly down the halls, I set about building a fire in the grate and stretch my feet out on a plush divan. I suspect Raleigh's arrival will throw the plans for tomorrow into disarray. My thoughts drift to the Earl of Clanricarde. Neither of my husbands would've travelled in the dead of night to reunite with me, but he's just the sort of man who I could see doing that.

I scoff at the ridiculous thought. My imagination is running wild and I'm halfway to hero worshipping him, all because he rescued me once before. Had I not freed him from my husband's prison first? Perhaps, he did it to repay the debt. I shouldn't be thinking about him.

Bess and her husband emerge from their locked bedchamber the following afternoon. The rosiness in her cheeks tells me it was time well spent.

"We shall have our sleigh ride tomorrow. A fitting way to celebrate Christmas Eve," she promises her guests. No one is disappointed. Outside the wind is howling, hardly the day for venturing outdoors.

Sir Walter Raleigh's return provides excitement enough. He takes centre stage as an admiring crowd of onlookers gathers near him. He begins by recounting tales from his sea voyage and then reads a poem he's been working on.

"It's half-finished and hardly worthy of being heard," he says, with false humbleness. There's no one now living that can compete with his talent.

"Does poetry displease you?" Richard asks me in a hushed whisper.

I realise I've been scowling. Taking greater care to

arrange my face into one of contentment, I shake my head. "It's not poetry nor Sir Walter's stories. My mind was wandering into the past."

"Those pesky memories of yours," he says, teasing with a shake of his head. "I shall strive to make you forget them."

I flush pink. What could he mean by that? There's no time for me to ask, even if I was brave enough to do so.

CHAPTER 2

T he heavy mantle weighs me down as I make my
way through the yard to the waiting sleighs.
Servants have cleared most of the snow away, but the
compacted snow and ice that remains is still a hazard.
The quilted doublet and wool undercoat I wear do little
to protect me against the chill.

Still, the rest of the guests are undaunted by the
prospect of spending the day outside. As I get closer, I
can see why. Hot bricks are being laid on the floor of the
sleigh, with blankets and furs piled high. Many have
already found their seats. Bess waves me over and her
husband relinquishes her long enough to allow her to
greet me properly.

"You'll be sitting with us," she says.

"Are you sure I wouldn't be in the way?" I ask, eyeing
the amorous Raleigh.

"Nonsense. There's four to a carriage anyway," Bess
says, with a twinkle in her eye. Raleigh's arms wrap

around his wife's waist and pull her back. "Next time we shall have to order more so we may enjoy some privacy."

I glance at my feet as Bess giggles.

"Can I help you get into the sleigh, Lady Frances?"

I whip around to find Lord Richard standing there looking sheepish. He looks handsome in his rich green velvet coat.

"I–" I say, about to refuse, when I catch the challenge in his eyes. "Yes, thank you."

I expect him to hold out his hand to me, but instead, his hands move to my waist and lift me up into my seat with one fluid motion.

Raleigh laughs and says, "careful, Richard. Soon all the ladies will demand to be lifted into their carriages and not all of us are as strong as you."

"My lord, that was unnecessary," I say rather breathlessly.

He is unrepentant as he shrugs. "On the contrary, it was efficient." He leaps up and sits beside me. It's not long before everyone has settled and Raleigh gives the signal to head out. Each sleigh is pulled by two enormous draft horses. As we reach the open field outside the estate, the sleighs fan out and the horses pick up speed. Suddenly we are flying over the field and I am filled with a childish glee. I try my best not to notice as we get jostled around how Richard's body presses against my own. Once when I nearly fall forward, he catches me. Bess looks thrilled and not just with the ride and the return of her husband.

I will have to assure her there's nothing going on

between the two of us, but I doubt she would believe me.

I lean back in my seat, looking up at the crisp blue sky, amazed by the dazzling beauty all around.

All too soon, we are returning to the house with our rosy cheeks and hearts racing from the adventure. As we disembark from the sleighs and are no longer protected by the added furs and blankets, I start to shiver against the cold. I'm not alone as we all rush inside to where the servants have built up huge fires in the gallery over-looking the inner courtyard. We are treated to a pair of acrobats tumbling in the snow below as we enjoy steaming cups of spiced wine. I close my eyes, breathing in the heady scent of cinnamon and cloves and let out a long sigh.

"Are you well?" Bess asks. "I know I've been neglectful."

I laugh. "Quite the opposite. I am deliriously happy. As for neglecting me, I suppose I can occasionally share you with your husband." I nudge her with my elbow.

She flushes as she says, "we are trying to make the most of our time together." I follow her gaze to where her husband is hoisting their young son on his shoulders so he can see the acrobats. "He's come without permission. The queen is surely to hear he has returned to England's shore and will send for him or command him to return to Jersey."

I squeeze her hand, trying to comfort her.

"Anyway, I came to ask you about the Earl of Clan-ricarde."

"What is there to ask?" I feel myself stiffen.

"I've seen the way he looks at you and this morning..."

I roll my eyes and whisper, "Bess, you made up the seating arrangements. You all but forced him to sit beside me and interact with me."

Her devious smirk tells me she knows something I don't. I watch her, debating whether or not to tell me. Finally she says, "he asked to be placed beside you."

I try to ignore the flutter in my chest at the revelation.

"It's clear to me he likes you."

"He's an earl," I say, pointing out the obvious. "I'm likely some passing fancy to him. You started out this Christmas season with romantic notions about my prospects, and your husband's return has only made things worse. I'm realistic..."

Bess cuts me off with a look. "Don't pretend you don't feel the same. At the very least, admit you are slightly interested in him. He's the only one you've really spent any time with. Do you think I invited all the single eligible men that I knew here for my benefit? You've only danced with one of them."

"Your son is asking for you," I say, noticing the blonde-haired boy waving towards her. He's nine now, the spitting image of his father. However, the similarities end there. He has neither the patience nor willingness to learn. Since I've arrived, he's been content to spend his days escaping his tutors in favour of strutting around the estate, ordering around the servants. They tolerate him for love of Bess and Walter, but I bet many of them pray he will change as he grows. In the past Bess had been stricter, but the loss of her firstborn son has made her protective and indulgent of the second.

"Please excuse me," Bess says. "Don't think you can escape this discussion."

I nod, knowing I wouldn't be so lucky. With a swish of her gown, she is gone. As I watch Bess doting on her son, my heart aches for my own children. I've been lucky. The queen has been generous in arranging places for them. They will receive a brilliant education and perhaps, one day soon, I can bring them together under one roof. I brush away this sentimental thought.

For the rest of the day, I take care to avoid Richard. I don't want to give anyone the wrong impression.

"Lady Frances, we need a fourth," Lord Humphrey calls out. I turn to find him sitting at a card table. Lady Mary and Lord Gilbert there already. "Will you join us?"

An odd anxiety gnaws at me, but I nod and with a courtly smile take my seat amongst them.

Lord Humphrey deals out the cards with efficiency.

"Shall we make this game more interesting?" Lord Gilbert asks, picking up his cards. He's an infamous gambler.

"We could," Lord Humphrey says. Across from him, Lady Mary grins.

There's a twist in my stomach as I say, "Unfortunately, I cannot partake in games of chance. I don't have a fortune to lose..."

"It would be my honour to lend you what you need," Lord Humphrey says, interrupting me. "And you cannot refuse me."

My lips part ready to do just that when he meets my eyes and says, "you wouldn't wish to ruin our fun, would you? We will set limits. There's no sense starting the New Year in debt."

Lord Gilbert grunts by way of agreement though I see the disappointment twist his smile into a frown.

We play for two hours. The ebbs and flow of the game keep my mind occupied and I laugh as Lord Humphrey slides over my winnings.

"You should've warned us you were such an adept player," he says, his eyes flashing.

"And miss out on all this fun," I say, a triumphant smile on my face.

"If you are done making moon eyes at each other, let's play another hand," Lord Gilbert huffs. I swallow hard as I give him a sidelong look. His cheeks are a rosy pink from the spirits he's been drinking all night. He picks up the small glass beside him and, with a disappointed sigh, looks behind him. A servant comes forward.

"Can't you see this is empty? Did I not tell you to keep it full? My throat is so dry," he says, complaining.

Lady Mary places a hand on his shoulder while I share a look of amusement with Lord Humphrey.

"Don't worry about him," he says, leaning towards me. "He's a sore loser."

The next round we play, I strategically lose a few hands. The tidy pile of winnings I'd won is whittled down to a few coins. Gilbert seems happy to have recovered some of his losses. He even is generous enough to pat my hand. "Next time I shall show you a few of my techniques, Lady Frances. Don't despair over a bit of bad luck."

I have to bite the inside of my cheek to hold back my smile as I thank him for his kindness. Then I return the coins Humphrey lent me.

"There's no need, Lady Frances," he says.

I know a man of his fortune wouldn't even blink at losing a few shillings, but I insist. "I'd hate to feel indebted to anyone, even over a paltry sum."

Lady Mary snickers. That uneasy feeling in the pit of my stomach returns. Impoverished as I am, I no longer belong here. But Lord Humphrey smiles. "We could all learn a thing or two from you."

The game breaks up and I wander over to Bess, who's watching her husband play a game of chess with Lord Richard.

"You look like you were having fun," Bess says. "Why did you leave?"

"Games of chance don't hold the same joy for me they once did."

Bess tuts. "And the company?"

Richard's eyes flick to mine for a brief moment before returning to the board.

"There was nothing wrong with the company," I say. What can Bess be meaning by this line of questioning in front of Richard and her husband, of all people?

Raleigh, catching on to his wife's intentions faster

than I do, admonishes her. "Bess, you cannot trap your friend into insulting your guests."

"Perhaps, next time, the lady should try her hand at games of strategy," Lord Richard says, not looking up as he moves a pawn forward to capture Raleigh's knight.

On Christmas day, I rise early with Bess and follow her to the great hall where she oversees the final decorations being put up for the feast. Applewood will burn all day filling the hall with its sweet scent. Tinsel decorates the walls, and rich tapestries are brought out of storage. Together with the evergreens, the house is transformed. Pleased at last with the arrangements, we return to Bess' room where I help her put the final flourishes on her outfit for the day. I catch her watching me as I tie the ribbon of her sleeves in place.

"Why are you looking at me like that?" I ask.

"Just thinking how well you'd look in my crimson gown with a garland of holly in your hair."

I laugh. "Really, Bess. I could not and you cannot dress me like some young maiden. Do you forget I am thirty-five? It would be unseemly."

She clicks her tongue on the roof of her mouth in displeasure. "Perhaps you are right. It wouldn't be proper today, but on the last day of twelfth night the rules are thrown out the window. You'll have all your suitors chasing after you then."

"Are you so eager to see me married off? I don't think

my parents worked so hard to get rid of me. If I've over-stayed my welcome, just say so," I tease.

Bess wraps her arms around my middle, pulling me into a tight hug. "Nonsense. But I wish to see you smile again and feel secure. I know that's what has you tossing and turning at night."

I am touched. "I will admit that I've been enjoying myself more than I thought. Your friends are kind."

"Lord Humphrey especially?" she asks with another giggle, as if she cannot help herself.

"Not only him. I was apprehensive at first to mingle in society. Regardless of their true feelings, your guests are content to keep their opinions to themselves and have been as welcoming as I could've hoped for."

"So you aren't the social pariah you believe yourself to be?"

"Among your carefully selected friends? No, I suppose not," I say, with the hint of a smile.

Bess returns to her looking glass and adds the final touches to her outfit. The rings she wears on her fingers outshine the string of pearls and rubies she wears at her neck.

I step back to admire her. "Your husband won't be able to take his eyes off you." My hand goes to my own bare neck without thinking. There was a time not too long ago where such finery would've been mine as well. However, jewellery brought me no joy when my husband was neglecting me to carouse with his mistresses.

Bess looks over her shoulder at me and then opens

her jewellery box. She pulls out a delicate chain of gold with a square-cut emerald pendant.

"You should wear this tonight," she says, holding it out to me.

"Your generosity has been too great already," I say with a shake of my head.

"It's a loan, so think nothing of it."

Before I can protest further, she clasps it around my neck and pats my cheek.

"You must allow me to be charitable to you. How could I forget how you stood by me when the queen discovered my marriage to Sir Walter? Even my brother refused to speak to me. You didn't turn me away, did you? No. In fact, if I recall correctly, you lent me a great deal of money."

I give her a weary smile. "Then I shall be gracious and accept your generosity now."

We join the rest of the party in the hall. Everyone is in high spirits as we attend Mass. The chapel has been brightly lit. The words of the priest are uplifting. As we exit the church, the ringing of bells serenades us.

The ladies retreat to a private parlour. No one is allowed to work over the festive season, so neither of us touches our needlework. We spend the hour resting and gossiping. It's here I learn that Arabella Stuart has incurred the wrath of the Queen once again.

"She insists she never even spoke the Earl of Hertford," Lady Joan says, her tone implying she didn't believe this. The others giggle.

"I feel inclined to believe her. The man is rather shameless," I say, without thinking.

The ladies turn to me with a grin.

"Oh?" Lady Joan arches her brow, inviting me to speak.

I wonder if it would've been best to remain in the background. Anything I say can be used against me later on.

"He first married Katherine Grey, in secret did he not? Then a Howard heiress. Lord Edward seems keenly ambitious in his choice of wives. Of course, he'd be chasing after another lady of royal blood. I don't see why a sixty-year-old man would appeal to a lady like Lady Arabella. Surely, she has more sense."

"You are her great defender," Lady Joan says, the hint of a smile on her lips.

"Merely pointing out the obvious. If she were to engage in some scandalous marriage, it would not be with him."

"I suppose we must rely on your expertise in such matters. You were married twice in secret yourself, much to the displeasure of the queen," she says.

"Hush, Lady Joan." Lady Mary springs to my defence. "You are just bitter no one ever found you appealing enough to try to get under your skirts. Your father had to tempt a mere knight with a hefty dowry to marry you."

Bess, who was sipping on some wine, chokes on a laugh as she struggles to keep from spilling the contents all over herself.

I rush over to take the cup from her and hand her a kerchief to wipe her mouth.

When Bess composes herself, she looks at the wide-eyed ladies assembled around the room. "Not one lady here is innocent. We've all had our share of indiscretions. However, let me settle one matter here once and for all. Of all of us assembled here, I am the most scandalous creature."

That breaks the tension and we all laugh.

"Perhaps we can have some music," she says. "Lady Joan, will you honour us?"

Her vanity stroked, Lady Joan stands and wanders over to the virginals. She holds her head high as she sits down and plays. To her credit, she is a skilled musician.

CHAPTER 3

At last we gather in the hall for a grand Christmas dinner. I had foolishly forgone eating anything in the morning and now my stomach churns at the tantalising scent of roasted meats drifting up from the kitchens.

As we take our seats, I find myself seated at the table opposite of Lord Richard. I can't help but admire the beautiful cut of his cream-coloured suit. His eyes meet mine from across the room. I've been caught staring. Again. My cheeks flush as Sir Walter stands, glass in hand to make a toast.

"I can hear your stomachs rumbling over the music, so I shall be brief. I wish to let you know how grateful I am you were able to come celebrate this Christmas season with us. Let us raise our cups to give thanks for Queen Elizabeth's health and England's continued prosperity."

We drink deep and Sir Walter waves for the servants

to come forward. They carry in heavily laden trays of food.

The first dish set before me is figgy pudding. I take a spoonful. The fragrant mixture of ground up almonds, ginger, honey and figs bathes my tongue in sweetness. I admit I eat it faster than can be considered ladylike.

As quickly as they appeared, the bowls disappear. The sound of beating drums at the entrance of the hall has everyone turning to watch as the next dish comes forward.

The steward of the household has the honour of carrying in the boar's head. The old man strains against the weight, but he neither trips nor waivers as he parades it around the room so we can all admire the opulence on the platter. We applaud as it is set down at the head table for Sir Walter to carve and dole out portions to all his guests. The steward bows and retreats.

Halfway through the dinner, four men dressed all in black wearing black masks trapeze into the hall. They declare they are holding the rest of the food hostage unless we can find some way to defeat them.

Sir Walter declares he will duel them all, but as he leaps forward, they dance away.

"Only love can sway us," one shouts.

From the alcoves come four of Bess' ladies-in-waiting dressed in gauzy gowns of virginal white. The musicians play a galliard. With a laugh, Sir Walter retreats as they pair off and dance.

Once the hearts of the cruel knights are melted by love, the feast can safely resume.

"You should've danced, Lady Frances. You are far more graceful than they were," Lord Humphrey says, on my left. I say nothing to his flattery. "I hope you will agree to be my partner later on."

"I cannot promise to be in any state to dance after this meal, but if I am, I shall."

More rich dishes follow, from quails served in a reduced wine sauce to roast venison stuffed with herbs and raisins. By the time the servants bring out Christmas pies, I am stuffed. My hand goes to my stomach as I stare at the piece placed before me. The crust is thick and buttery. The scent of nutmeg and cinnamon is equally tempting yet, I cannot fathom taking a bite.

As I look around, it is clear I am not alone. Only Sir Walter Raleigh has the energy to keep us entertained. With the lilting sound of music in the background, he recounts his adventures in the new world. Once he grows bored with that, he sets about dramatizing his naval battles with the Spanish and how he pirated their treasure.

At last there is music, and Bess invites us to dance. Slowly but surely those of us who can rise to our feet. As promised, I allow Lord Humphrey to lead me out for the first dance. Far from being graceful, I feel sluggish and it takes two more dances for me to fully recover.

As the fourth dance begins, I excuse myself. Wandering over to one of the many alcoves in the hall, I take a moment to rest alone on a cushioned bench.

It's not long before a shadow is cast on the wall in front of me and I crane my neck to see who it is. Richard

Burke is standing there with a sheepish smile on his face. One hand grasps the back of his neck.

"Apologies, Lady Frances. I was just wandering by when I caught sight of you. I hadn't meant to intrude."

"Not at all." I hear myself saying.

"Are you tired?" He asks, gently.

"No," I say, wondering if it was even more sinful to lie on Christmas day. I simply wish for him to stay.

"Then I'd like to take you back to the dancefloor."

I put a hand over my heart in mock surprise. "It sounds as if you plan to abduct me."

"Something like that," he says, his smile deepening. He holds out his hand towards me and I allow him to pull me to my feet.

As the music carries us away, I feel my exhaustion melt away to be replaced by joy.

I don't recall when I retired for the night, but I awake in the morning with a pounding headache and feet so sore that I'm not sure I can leave my bed.

Maids bring in basins of scalding hot water for me to wash in. They place one basin before me and I soak my feet in the scented water. I let out a sigh at how good that feels and settle back to let them brush out my long hair.

After a time, a maid clears her throat and gently reminds me the household is expected at church soon. It strikes me just how long I've been sitting here daydreaming. Jumping to my feet with a wince, I hurry to get dressed, forgoing any formal gown that would take longer to put on for a plain dress. I hope everyone sees it as my desire to appear pious.

As we process to the church, we each carry gifts to hand out to the needy. The few coins I have disappear into the hands of poor widows and children. Bess and Walter donate bolts of cloth and sacks of grain. They also distribute a heavy purse of gold to be distributed among the community. I only wish I could do more.

After we enter the church and listen as the priest preaches about the importance of charity and generosity. My hand drifts to my neck when, with a look of horror, I realise it's bare. I've left the necklace from Bess somewhere. As we head back to the house, I pray it's in my bedchamber, otherwise I do not know where it could be.

"Can I help you, Lady Frances?"

I cover my mouth to muffle the yelp that would inevitably draw more attention to myself. Looking up, I find Lord Richard peering down at me, eyes full of concern.

I get to my feet, brushing the dust off my skirts as best I can.

"I was looking for something," I say. What must he think of me crawling about on all fours like a child?

"Clearly," he says, with a cough. "I'd hardly assume a lady of your stature would be —." He stops and I believe I catch a faint blush on his cheeks. "What were you looking for? Perhaps I could be of service."

I am about to stubbornly refuse, but that'd be foolish.

"A necklace. I thought I had left it in my room, but it's not there. The clasp must have opened or somehow broken last night. It's not mine, so I'm desperate to find it," I say.

"And what does this necklace look?"

"Why?"

He gives me a smile. "I must know what it looks like if I am to help you find it."

My mouth opens, ready with a protest before I snap it shut. "You are too kind. Thank you. I hope I am not keeping you from something?"

He laughs. "You are saving me from another round of billiards."

"That doesn't sound so terrible," I say.

"It is. Every time you lose a point you must drink a cup of wine."

"Ah. So everyone will have drunk themselves into a stupor by the afternoon."

"A fate I'm eager to escape," he says, looking around the hall. It was such a desolate place with all the furniture tucked away. "I assume you are retracing your steps."

"I even checked the corridor on the way here. The necklace is a gold chain with an emerald pendant."

"You asked the servants? Perhaps, it was swept up if it fell during the dinner."

"You think they pocketed it?"

He gave a shrug. "I wouldn't blame them for taking the opportunity, but I was going to suggest asking Lady Bess if they returned it to her. Should we not ask her?"

Not having considered that possibility, I blanch. "I'd rather not trouble her."

"Ah, it is her necklace." He gives me a reassuring smile. "Don't worry, your secret is safe with me."

We scour the hall. Then a thought strikes me and I hurry to the alcove where I sat looking out the window at the night sky. The shutters are closed, and it's hard to see in the dim light. At first I'm disappointed, but as I kneel to look under the bench, a glint of gold catches my eye. I reach for it and pull it out.

I found it. Clutching the necklace to my chest, I say a silent prayer in thanks.

"You have it," Richard says, coming up behind me.

"You sound disappointed. Why?" I arch a brow.

He laughs. "You are far too perceptive. You see, I was hoping to be the one to discover it and thus, become your knight in shining armour."

I hold out my hand to him, and without hesitation, he helps me to my feet. "I enjoyed your company."

"I'm glad to hear that, Lady Frances," he says, a smile tugging at the corners of his lips. "I can't help but think you've been avoiding me."

"Nonsense."

"Then it's simply that you prefer the company of others over mine."

I take a step back from him. My eyes roam over him from head to toe, trying to understand what he means by this. "My lord, that sounds like a very personal question."

"I will be frank with you, my lady. By now you must have realised how much I admire you. I wish to spend more time getting to know you, but if you don't feel the same then I won't trouble you again."

"Admire me?" I parrot back, incredulous.

"You sound surprised."

Not wishing to disparage myself, I merely shrug. "You are quite a catch and I would never presume a man such as yourself would look twice at me." Then I flush and add rather boldly, "with honourable intentions, that is."

"You must not have been around many honourable men then," he says, with a low rumble of displeasure in his voice.

"I suppose I have been unlucky in that regard." I tilt my head, watching him. "How can I give you an answer? We don't know each other very well. If I confess I like you, then you may change your mind after getting to know me better. Think of how embarrassing that would be." I twist the gold chain around my fingers, wondering at my daring.

Amusement and hope flicker in his eyes. "You are right. Clearly, I've made a grave mistake. I should cut my losses."

Seeing he has no intention of leaving, I chuckle. "Yet you seem undeterred."

My heart hammers in my chest as he steps towards me. There's a delicious look in his eye, and I desperately want him to kiss me. The thought both terrifies and excites me.

"I never took you for the sort of woman who would torment a man with teasing." He covers my hand in his. "I want us to speak plainly now. Would you be interested in getting to know me better?"

Those blue eyes of his are filled with an intensity that sends a shudder down my spine.

"Yes."

He smiles then, recalling himself steps away from me. Clearing his throat he says, "we should return to the party."

I nod.

"Will you accompany me for a walk around the gardens tomorrow?"

"If my duties permit me. There's much to do and I promised Lady Bess I'd help her."

He tilts his head to hide his disappointment. "I understand."

"Tomorrow she plans for us to dance the day away. I hope you shall whisk me off my feet again."

"Without fail."

"Good."

He offers me his arm and escorts me to where the rest of the party has gathered. There is great laughter as we watch Sir Walter Raleigh pour a fortune of Burgundian wine and brandy into a wide rimmed bowl. He takes a plate of almonds, figs and raisins from a servant and mixes it in.

"And now for the grand finale," he says, in his loud

booming voice. He lights a taper and, approaching the bowl, sets it alight. Bright blue flames spread around the bowl. Their never-ending dance is mesmerising.

"Who will be the first?"

The men all nudge each other forward. Snap-dragon, is a dangerous game. The goal is to fetch a treat out of the bowl without getting burned. An impossible task made even harder by the starched frills at the end of our sleeves.

One look at Bess' pursed lips tells me how much she disapproves. She goes pale when she sees her eager son push forward to show how brave he is.

Thankfully, his father intervenes.

Two guests try but fail. We applaud them for their bravery. It is then that Richard steps forward. I wonder what he thinks he's playing at. Struggling to get a look, I stand on my tiptoes. He seems to study the bowl carefully, murmuring something to Sir Walter, who grins up at him. Then, with a quick sweeping motion, he plucks a fig from the bowl.

"Watch out for the carpet," Bess calls out.

Indeed, the fig is drenched in wine, and Richard is having a hard time keeping it from spilling. More line up to have a go but he retreats back to my side.

"How are you holding on to the fig?" I ask, peering at it in his palm.

He rips it in half and offers me a piece. "Try it. It's quite cool. I daresay the brandy has improved the taste somewhat."

"Thank you," I say, popping it into my mouth. The

brandy mixed with the fig juices burns going down my throat. "You don't like figs?"

"I try to avoid them when I can. But they are the easiest thing to pick out. Most go for the almonds or raisins. Their small size and slipperiness increases your chance of getting burned. Here." He offers me the last piece. "Seeing how much you enjoy it; I feel my efforts were well worth it."

"You also got the chance to show off your prowess and fearlessness," I say, wincing as someone yelps as they pull their hand away from the bowl. The next person succeeds.

Richard grins. "Of course."

Curiosity getting the better of me, I cannot help but ask, "what is your trick?"

"It's all about speed and choosing your target. The fig was also near the edge of the bowl, so there was less chance I'd get singed."

"Still seems like a foolish game. I hope my son wouldn't risk injuring himself for a few treats."

"That's what the Christmas season is all about," he begins to say, then catching my worried expression amends. "But I am sure he will come to no harm. He might even have more sense than me and not partake."

That earns him a half-hearted smile. From the corner of my eye, I catch Bess watching us, and I have to fight my first instinct to move away from Richard.

"May I see you tomorrow?"

"We are both guests here. It's likely you will."

"Let me be more specific. Will you take a stroll with me in the gardens?"

I arch a brow. "To admire the roses?"

He laughs. "The hedges, at least, are evergreen."

Taking pity on him, I touch his forearm. "After all this feasting, I yearn for some fresh air. I'd be happy to have you escort me around the gardens."

"After Matins then?"

I incline my head as I draw away and move to join Bess.

CHAPTER 4

B ess has the decency not to question me when she catches me dressing for to go outside.

"Don't lose track of time," she says, with a wink as she hands me a furred muff.

She leaves before she can see the way my cheeks redden.

I'm not doing anything wrong though and with that thought, I march myself outside. Today is a mild winter's day with the sun shining brightly overhead, melting the snow. My heavy leather boots come in handy on the icy pathways.

He's there waiting for me. The surprise on his face when he sees me makes me yearn to kiss away his worries. A thought I quickly shake away.

"Lady Frances, I was wondering if you'd come," he says, greeting me with a bow.

"You are lucky the wonderful weather tempted me

outdoors," I say, teasing. "I'm not likely to go back on my word."

"Neither am I," he says, stepping forward and offering me his arm.

We wander the shovelled path of the hedge maze. The beauty all around me leaves me breathless. The green of the hedges is striking against the fresh snow. It's not often I venture outdoors in winter, something I'm regretting now.

"You are quite dazzled," he says, in a low whisper. "I wish I could take the credit."

Chuckling, I say, "I suppose I have you to thank for this. Unlike Bess, I am not much of an outdoors woman. I learned to ride and hunt, but I never developed an appreciation for the outdoors."

"I suppose that's why she spent the better half of the previous night debating with me on which breed of horse is superior."

I nod. "She's become quite the expert on horses. Have you seen her stables? Many credit Sir Walter Raleigh with the quality of the steeds, but it's all her."

"It's admirable the way she's applied herself," he says. I like him all the more for accepting my words at face value.

We come to the centre of the maze, but rather than turn back, we take another exit. Conversation flows easily from banal topics regarding the celebrations to the growing price of wheat.

"The world has come to a standstill," I muse. "It's as

if everyone is waiting to see what will become of the English after the queen — God forbid, passes away."

"And I don't think most of them are wishing us well," Richard says, running a hand through his hair. "I fear that all the carefully laid plans for the succession will fall apart. It keeps me up at night."

"I had not realised you were so favoured at court that you were privy to such important plans."

He gives me a side-long look. "I know nothing for certain, but I do travel often around the country and am a friend of Robert Cecil's."

"So it will be King James of Scotland then?"

"He is the most obvious choice."

I think of Arabella Stuart and how hopeful she is. "Because England is tired of queens?"

"Because he is the strongest claimant."

"Interesting choice of words," I say.

"You shall not lead me into making treasonous remarks or assumptions, Lady Frances," he says with mock seriousness.

I laugh. "My skills must have grown rusty. My father would've been sad to hear I failed to entrap you. I suppose the King of Scotland is the only one with an army. I concede you are correct."

"A fine job I'm doing wooing you. I should be reading you poetry, not discussing politics."

"Trust me when I say I prefer the latter."

We round a corner and come out on to the snow-covered field. I raise a hand to shade my eyes from the blinding sun to get a better look. We've stumbled into a glittering dreamlike world. The stark white goes on for miles, framed by a hunting park to the left and the estate to the right. The strangest desire to run out on to the field strikes me. I want to break the smooth perfection of the snow's surface.

Instead, I sink back onto my heels and let out a sigh.

"It's strange how you can stumble upon such beauty by happenstance," Richard says, his voice barely audible, as though he doesn't want to break the spell the land has cast over us.

It's then I spy a small bird of prey circling over the field. I point to it and we watch as the kestrel hovers over a particular patch of snow. Then, with astounding speed, it dives. As it emerges from the flurry of white, I see it's captured a small mouse in its talons.

As it flies off with its catch, I place my hand in Richard's. We turn to face each other, my gaze travels from his warm eyes to his lips. A surge of desire washes over me. I find myself stepping closer.

He leans down, closing the distance between us. Instinctively, my eyes close. I feel his mouth hovering above my own, his breath fanning my face. Now is my chance to step away and end this madness. I don't. Instead, my grip tightens on his hand. He captures my lips in a sweet, gentle kiss before pulling away.

"I've been wanting to do that for a while," he says, his voice low and gravelly.

My heart is still racing and I wish he hadn't pulled

away. Clearing my throat, I force myself to say the proper thing. "We should probably return to the house."

For a moment, we both hesitate. Indecision leaves us frozen in place. Then the spell breaks and we spring apart.

At the house, we return just in time to watch the parade of the Lord of Misrule. A gardener by the name of Phillip Taylor, is dressed in a flamboyant green velvet suit patched with silver bells.

We watch him approach Sir Walter Raleigh, who is standing on the steps of the main entrance. Master Phillip kneels before him as though Sir Walter was a Bishop in a church.

We watch as, with great solemnity, Sir Walter places a crown of ivy and red berries on his head. Then he hands Master Phillip his sceptre, a spade decorated with greenery and more silver bells.

Master Phillip rises to his feet and raises his arms to give a great cheer. We all applaud as his lively court, also dressed in green, hoists him high into the air and parade him around the courtyard. Men go before the Lord of Misrule playing flutes and drums. We all bow as he passes. For the next few days, he will command the household.

As his first act, he declares that we should erect a snow fort. Much of this must have been planned ahead of time because they also erect a tent for the ladies to watch from. Hot braziers are brought out and we enjoy chestnuts and hot ale. We cheer on the men as they work away with shovels and whatever else they can get their hands on to build a crude fort of snow and wood.

When the Lord of Misrule is satisfied, we bring roasted meat out as a reward for the workers. His courtiers play a merry tune and they invite us ladies to dance. As I twirl round, hand clasped with Bess, the tempo increases. We start tripping over each other, trying to keep up with the music. I join the others in laughing with wild abandon as it goes even faster.

The gentlemen rescue us from the musicians by pelting them with snowballs, and we are free to stop.

That night I sleep like a stone, my mouth fixed into a permanent smile. I don't remember the last time I was ever so happy.

The next few days leading up to New Year's Day are spent hunting, putting on plays and playing games. When we aren't occupied with some activity, we are feasting on delicacies. Throughout it all, Richard finds his way by my side. When we can, we slip away from the group to enjoy quiet conversations and more than a few stolen kisses.

One day Bess pulls me aside after chapel and demands to know everything.

"It hasn't escaped my notice how close the two of you have become," she says.

I flush and her eyes narrow, as if I've just confirmed all her suspicions. "We are getting to know one another."

"And that's all?" Her brow arches.

Before I can contradict her, she clasps her hands around mine. "Tell me truthfully. Have you fallen in love?"

"How can I answer that?" I try to pull away, but her grip is unrelenting.

"Does your heart ache for him when he's not around? Do you miss him every moment he's not with you?"

I look away and that is all the confirmation she needs. Bess lets out a girlish squeal. "Oh, Frances, I am so happy for you."

"Bess... really. It might all come to nothing."

She scoffs. "I've seen the way he looks at you. His eyes follow you around the room. He hangs on your every word. He is madly in love with you and I'm sure he will propose before long." She glances at me with suspicion. "Unless he already has."

"No," I say. "He hasn't. Though he's spoken of marriage."

Her grin returns.

"This might all just be the celebratory mood of the season. He may not wish to marry me. Really, he should find himself an heiress and make a proper alliance."

Bess rolls her eyes. "I'll bet you that gold necklace I lent you that he will ask you within the week."

"Very well," I say and we shake on it.

On New Year's Day everyone dresses in their best. I wear my green gown with the sleeves embroidered with gold thread. I admire the way it brings out the colour of my eyes in the looking glass. At last, carrying my gifts for Bess and Walter, I join the others.

At the end of the gallery, the Lord of Misrule sits on his throne while the rest of the household gathers before him. A large table has been laid out full of gifts. Bess and Sir Walter come forward, hand clasped.

"We have prepared little gifts for all of you," Sir Walter says. "We wish to thank you for helping us celebrate this wondrous season." Cheers go up around the room.

We line up by order of precedence with the servants going first. Each has also prepared a little present for their Lord and Lady. A small pastry, or perhaps, a work of embroidery. When it is my turn, I step forward, kiss the both of them on the cheek and present them with my gift: a small book of prayers I composed myself. Bess hands me a furred muff with a secret smile. When I place my hands inside it, I find a small brown parcel. I open it to find the gold necklace. My heart races as I wonder what this means. What does she know? She meets my eyes and gives me a small mischievous grin. Bowing, I step back and allow the next guest to approach.

My throat is dry when I feel his presence behind me.

"Frances," he whispers in my ear. "May I speak to you?"

I lick my lips, not looking behind me but giving a tiny

nod. Placing a hand gently at my elbow, he leads me out of the gallery to an empty corridor.

"Richard —" I begin to say but was at a loss for words.

His hand finds mine, and he brings it up to his lips to place an endearing kiss on my open palm. Those eyes of his peer into mine as though he wishes to unravel the secrets of my heart.

"I wish to speak to you about the future," he says. "Our future. Frances, you must know how fond of you I've become. I cannot bear to think of us apart. Will you consent to being my wife?"

My lips part in shock. "Richard, I would wish for nothing more, but I cannot."

He looks pained. "Why not?"

"The queen. She will never consent to our match. I've married twice already and faced her displeasure. I don't think she will be so forgiving a third time."

"Then I will speak to her," he says, urgently. "She can have no reason to refuse me."

I shake my head. "She doesn't like me and will see me unworthy of you. Which is the truth. My age alone should be enough for you to hesitate."

His lips remain set in a grim line of determination. "But if she were not a concern. If I were to obtain permission to wed you, would you?"

My breath hitches. "Of course."

His hand finds my waist and pulls me close. A second later, his mouth descends upon my own. "That is all I needed to hear. We will be married. No matter how long we have to wait."

I nod, leaning my head against his broad chest. Against my better judgement, I believe him. Hope wells in my chest.

He pulls out a small pouch from his pocket and places it in my hand.

I look up, blinking in surprise.

"Open it," he urges.

Carefully unwrapping it, I am stunned to find a beautiful necklace of pearls strung on a silver chain.

"Richard, it's stunning," I say. It's all too much.

"I'm glad you like it. It will always remind me of this wintery season and the first time my lips touched your own at the edge of that snow-covered field."

Warmth spreads through my chest at his words. I reach up, my fingers bury themselves into his thick hair. A low hum of approval is all I need to press my lips against his.

We return to the long gallery. I hope no one notices my flushed cheeks and red lips.

That night, Bess sneaks into my bedchamber wrapped in a thick robe.

"So?" she says, her tone full of anticipation.

In reply, I hand her back the gold necklace. She looks shocked.

"What is this?"

"We are not getting married."

"B-but," she sputters incredulously.

"At least not yet," I say with a laugh. "He will try to

get the queen's approval first. Until then, we will continue on as we have."

"But what if she doesn't? What if there are delays?" Bess is outraged.

"Bess, as much as I care for him, I will not rush head-first into danger. If he cares for me as much as I care for him, then he will wait for me."

Her lips purse into a tight line of displeasure. "Very well."

"You may give me the necklace on the day of my wedding," I say. "I hope it shall be soon, for I admire it very much." This makes her laugh, and she embraces me before returning to her husband's bed.

As Twelfth Night arrives, there's a sense of sadness that the holiday season is coming to a close. Richard and I sit side by side, playing a game of cards. We go through the motions but aren't really paying attention.

"I shall leave for London after Mass tomorrow," he says.

"Won't you stay for the banquet after?"

"I would rather not delay for a single moment longer. You will remain with Bess until summer?"

I smile and incline my head. "Unless she grows bored with me and throws me out."

"Then I shall visit you here as often as I can."

Under the card table, our fingertips touch. I want to take everything I said back. How can I go on in this state

47

of secrecy and anticipation? Perhaps, we should have married in secret. I blink and force myself to set aside my impatience.

"Frances, it's your turn," he says, pointing to the cards in my hands. A knowing smile dancing across his features. Insufferable man.

A gentle summer breeze sweeps over me. I take a moment to stop and savour the sweet smell in the air.

There's something tranquil about me as I meander through the apple orchards of Sir Walter Raleigh's estate. His wife has invited me to stay for the summer months and I am happy to be in the company of such a lively woman. We spend our days walking through gardens, or riding in the deer park. In the evenings, we sew by the fire as we entertain ourselves with lively debates and giggle like young girls over gossip from the court.

I am no longer as young as I used to be, but neither have I withered away. With age has come wisdom and acceptance. I discover I can forgive the men I married for not loving me as completely as I would have wished. Considering the outcome, it was for the best. Love cannot be forced, it must be given willingly.

There is perhaps another secret reason why I am so at peace.

When I open my eyes again, I see him standing at the other end of the lane, regarding me with a lopsided smile.

"Lady Frances, good day," he calls out.

I raise my hand in greeting and study him as he approaches me.

"Good day, Lord Richard. What brings you here this day?"

"A Faerie Queene," he says, presenting me with a bouquet of wildflowers he had concealed behind his back.

I tut at him. "Should the queen have heard you say that..." Then I shake my head. "What will become of you?" I step closer to him. My gloved hand on his.

He casts a glance around us.

"We are alone," I reassure him.

He hums and tilts my chin up to meet his searching glance. "This is most improper, my lady."

A sly smile spreads across my face as I'm drawn closer by his entrancing eyes. "I am grateful that such a great knight is here to protect my virtue." The flowers he holds fall to the ground as I close the distance and press my lips against his own.

His arms wrap around me as he attempts to bite back a moan. The kisses alternate between sweet caresses and pressing desire. At last Richard pulls away, though he doesn't release me from his hold.

"We cannot keep going on like this my darling,

Frances," he whispers. "Have you thought about my proposal?"

My mouth is dry and for a moment I think of lying to him. But there is no lying to someone like Richard Burke, Earl of St. Albans and Clanricarde. "Every moment. You cannot imagine the temptation. But are you still sure? You deserve a far better marriage..."

He silences me with another kiss, nipping my bottom lip in disapproval. "Don't you dare say such things. I've wanted you since the moment you rescued me from that traitor's clutches."

"I never realised it until now but you were a damsel in distress."

"Indeed, I was even kept under lock and key." He bats his eyes at me and we cannot help but laugh. Then his expression grows serious. "You are the only one I want by my side. These secret meetings and stolen kisses — they aren't a game to me. If you will have me the king will give his blessing for this union."

"How do you know that?"

"I have already asked him."

"Tell me you haven't!" Richard cannot know what this means to me. If I agree this would be my first marriage conducted in the open.

"But I have. So you have no choice but to accept that you will be saddled with me until we both grow old and decrepit."

In shock, I swat his arm attempting to hide the joy blossoming in my chest. "Such sweet words and promises of the future. How can I say anything but yes?"

"How indeed..." He agrees, then stops to mid-sentence. "Though I wouldn't mind trying to convince you some more." Richard leans forward as if to kiss me again.

"You are incorrigible."

Our eyes lock as he holds me to him tighter than ever. "No. Insatiable."

AUTHOR'S NOTE

This story in an interlude between the ending of Countess of Intrigue and its epilogue.

There's no mention of how Frances met Richard Burke, so I have fabricated a possible set of events.

As we know, they lived a happy life together and had three children.

In this story, you also discover more of what happens with Walter Raleigh and his wife Bess. After Queen Elizabeth's death, he lost a great defender and would die as a traitor a few years later.

I've done extensive research on how the Tudors celebrated Christmas. The traditions might differ from our own, but I get the sense that the celebratory mood was the same. I also wouldn't mind twelve days of holidays. I hope you've enjoyed this short novella.

PREVIEW: PROLOGUE

Preview of my latest novel: The Lady's Fortune

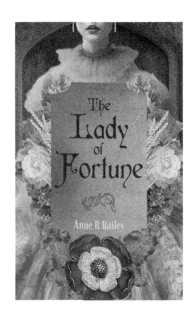

I t is hard to focus on threading my needle when a large beetle keeps colliding against the windowpane, desperate to escape.

Thud. Thud.

It sounds like it might injure itself in the attempt. I can understand its desperation. Who would want to be trapped in this miserable castle longer than necessary?

I envy the creature as it finally finds a crevice and flees. Would I ever leave? I was only seven years old, but I already knew my prospects were dim.

My hand smooths over the homespun wool of my skirt. I should be dressed in fine silks. After all, I am descended from two royal bloodlines—Plantagenet and York. But there is no money for finery anymore. Now we are grateful when we can keep a fire burning in the grate.

Long before I was born, my grandfather, the Duke of Buckingham, died on Tower Hill for threatening the king's power and, if rumours are true, seeking to claim the throne. His actions were nothing short of treason. So my father, instead of inheriting a dukedom and all the Stafford wealth, had to be content to walk away with his life.

I thought this was unfair. My parents had done nothing wrong, but I hadn't been there to complain. Not that anyone would have listened.

Everywhere I look, I see hints of a glorious past, from the faded tapestries to the heraldic symbols carved into stone. I know there are trunks and chests in the cellar containing court dresses and rich linens tucked away as we wait for better times. My parents are still proud of their heritage and dream of returning to court. They cling to the little that remains, but for how much longer can we go on? Every year, we are forced to sell our precious heirlooms to ensure we have food in our bellies. After the last remnants of our glory are gone, what will become of us?

Last spring, when the roof leaked, my mother's diamond necklace was used to pay for the repairs and outstanding debts to the crown. If the crops fail this year or some other tragedy befalls us, will we be able to find something of value to sell? Worry gnaws at me.

"Daydreaming, again?"

I snap out of my thoughts to see my mother peering down at me.

"Working." I hold up the embroidery I have been struggling with. A pattern of red roses shines against the beige cloth.

Her lips purse into a thin line of disapproval. "You were supposed to be practicing stitches."

The tightness in her tone warns me she is upset.

"I know. I just thought I could copy the pattern on your petticoat. The one you wore last Christmas. It was so beautiful and..."

Her finger runs over my work. I know it isn't perfect. Far from it. I haven't quite mastered the loops and tight stitches required to make the roses. Nor do I think I used the right colours for the leaves and shading.

"If you insist on jumping ahead in your lessons, then you shall keep working until you achieve perfection. Pull out every stitch and begin again."

"But mother—" The protest dies on my lips at her pinched expression. Today is not the day to argue with her.

She takes a seat close to the window and picks up her own needlework.

We are a large family and, judging from the swell of my mother's belly, we will grow even larger. I might be the fourth of seven children, but as one of two daughters, I am a rarity. My eldest sister's poor eyesight keeps her confided to the nursery and means I have our mother's undivided attention and tutelage.

At the moment, she is working on one of my father's linen shirts. I envy the intricate black embroidery stitched neatly into the collar. It is my mother's own work, something she learned years ago at the court of Queen Catherine. I am desperate for her to teach me. But even if she wasn't angry with me right now, black thread is expensive and there is no money for such frivolity.

For a time, we work side by side in silence until the sun begins to dip on the horizon. With it comes the noise and bustle of the household preparing for the evening. We hear the clattering of hooves and the shouts of my two older brothers as they ride into the courtyard with my father in tow. By now, they should've been sent to a great noble house to complete their education. But who would be foolish enough to befriend a family tainted by treason? What benefit could there be to allying with a struggling family?

My mother sets down her own needle and looks over

at me. I have finished taking out the stitches. My fingers, quick and nimble, undid what had been hours of needlework.

"Go get ready for supper and tell Margaret to come down as well." My mother dismisses me.

I almost protest, but when I blink, I feel the strain in my eyes. Even my back is stiff from sitting for so many hours. There is something pensive in the way she tilts her head to look out the window. As I leave, I catch her sad expression as she rubs her belly and continues to stare out at the darkening sky outside.

Every moment of our lives is laced with regret and bitterness. The knowledge of what could've been is a hard pill to swallow. Even for me.

Two days later, we receive an unexpected visitor.

My aunt, the Duchess of Norfolk, slides from her horse with a confidence and ease any knight would envy. She stares at us, arranged as we are in the courtyard, with pity. Only when her gaze settles on her brother does she smile.

With less than a year between them, they were inseparable in their early years. A tight bond had grown between them that distance and time could not rip asunder.

He steps forward, bidding her welcome to his home. A few years ago, she would have been giving him precedence. But now she is a duchess, and he is a mere lord with barely a penny to his name.

Her sharp critical gaze softens. "Harry, you don't need to be so formal with me," she says, as she steps forward and kisses both his cheeks before moving on to embrace my mother.

"Are you travelling north?" my mother asks, observing the retinue that accompanies my aunt. "I thought you'd be entrenched in London."

"As it happens, I am returning to Suffolk for a time. We shall speak more inside, where we won't be overheard," she says, her eyes catching mine.

Both my parents spin around and frown at me.

My cheeks redden as my aunt approaches.

"There is nothing wrong with listening in on others' conversations. Provided you don't get caught." At that, she chucks me under my chin.

I return her smile and curtsey to her, my movements graceful and the correct height for a lady of her rank.

"Well done," she says.

My mother hasn't failed to teach me courtly manners. At my side, I can feel Margaret stiffen. She is the quiet one, and I always steal the spotlight that rightfully belongs to her as the older sister. It isn't something I set out to do, and I am sorry if it bruises her pride to be overlooked.

That night, we dine in private, and after the meal is done, my father dismisses the servants. Finally, we are alone.

"Tell me, Margaret, do you play the virginals?" my aunt asks.

Margaret's cheeks go pink with pleasure as she nods.

"Will you play something for me now? I should dearly love to hear you."

"Of course." Margaret curtseys and rushes to get her instrument.

It isn't long before music fills the room. She might only be thirteen, but Margaret is already an accomplished musician. Before our family's disgrace, she delighted Queen Catherine with her playing and took lessons with Princess Mary.

The adults don't listen passively to her playing. They sit, heads pressed together, imparting news they don't wish to be overheard by spies at the keyhole. I am on my mother's left and do my best to keep still, hoping they will go on forgetting I am there.

"That whore has arranged my daughter's marriage," my aunt begins. "My poor Mary is to be wasted on Henry Fitzroy. I told my husband I would never agree to the match, but of course, my opinion counts for nothing." She lets out a heavy sigh. "And the poor queen... they keep moving her from castle to castle, each worse than the last. They aren't satisfied with stripping her of her dignity and titles. They are taking everything. Her jewels, her barge, her ladies-in-waiting. She's a prisoner, unable to see her daughter or the Spanish ambassador. It's disgraceful how she's being treated."

My aunt is speaking of Catherine of Aragon, the Spanish queen, whom the king is intent on divorcing. By all accounts, my aunt should support him. The Howards stand to gain untold wealth and influence at court if the king succeeds in casting her aside and marrying Anne Boleyn, her husband's niece. However, my aunt is loyal and holds strong convictions. Anne Boleyn might be her niece, but she is a mere knight's daughter. Even worse is the fact that the Boleyns are descended from merchants, hardly worthy of marrying royalty.

I imagine it torments my aunt that someone of Anne's low breeding is now set above her.

"So you took yourself away from court to show your displeasure?" my father asks, his eyes full of mirth.

My aunt's curt nod tells him everything. "The official reason is that I am preparing Mary's dowry and gathering some heirlooms from the coffers at Kenninghall."

"Something you could've asked a servant to do for you." My father shakes his head. "You are playing with fire. Wouldn't it be better if you befriended the future queen? Think of what you are risking by insulting her like this."

She gives him a scornful look.

"You shall not lecture me, Henry," she says, imperious. "Between the two of us, I am the one who still holds a title and isn't living in some decrepit castle."

That stings. My father's eyes narrow, but he recovers his good humour quickly. "You are welcome to find more suitable accommodations elsewhere," he dares her.

I wonder at my father's bravery. But then again, they are siblings and have needled and teased each other for decades.

"We do apologise for not being able to entertain you as befits your station," my mother says, happy to play the part of peacemaker.

"Nonsense. My niece's playing is lovely. Her breeding shows in her talent. It was a stroke of bad luck that you and yours are not where you belong. Once Anne loses the king's favour and is cast aside, perhaps he will see sense. He cannot continue promoting every lowborn person who can string together enough words to form a sentence." She bites her lower lip, casting a glance around the room to reassure herself we are alone.

I sit back in my seat, wondering who she is talking about. The conversation continues in hushed whispers, and even I can no longer hear them.

Margaret plays for half an hour before her fingers falter. It has been a long day. My mother nods to her to set aside her instrument and take a seat with us.

"I stopped by with another proposition in mind," my aunt says. "I want to offer to take Margaret and Dorothy. They shall join my household and be given a proper education. I shall arrange good marriages for them and bring them to court as often as is fitting."

My heart skips a beat. I cannot believe what she has just said. My eyes go wide as I glance from my parents to my aunt.

She chuckles. "This one is excited. Tell me Dorothy, do you dream of going to London? Bumping shoulders with the great people of this land?"

I can hear the mocking tone in her voice and lower my eyes.

Again, she chuckles. "I hope it never disappoints you, niece."

"Never," I say with such fervour that she is taken aback.

She glances at my father. "She will wilt if you keep her here tucked away in the country."

"It isn't by choice that we are living here like this." I hear the bitterness in his voice as he says this.

"Then let me help you."

He groans. "I wish you could speak to the king. Your husband, perhaps..."

"I know, Henry," she says, reaching over to pat his hand. "But I'm afraid even if my husband were inclined to help, it would be beyond his powers to get your titles and lands restored to you. I wish there was more I could do."

My mother dismisses us so the adults can speak freely without us children.

I have to pinch my wrist to hold back a protest. How can we be sent away at such a crucial time? I need to know if I am to become my aunt's maid-in-waiting. All my dreams might be within reach. On a whim, my aunt has changed the course of my destiny. I regard her in a new light. She is a powerful force unlike any I have ever encountered. What would it be like to wield that sort of influence? Then another more terrifying thought strikes me. What if she changes her mind?

For a while, it appears she has. The following day, my aunt leaves without a word to me or Margaret. My parents are in a contemplative mood but say nothing.

The news from London is bad and they worry war might come to England's shores. I hate the spark of hopefulness that bloomed in my heart last night. Will I never escape my dreary home?

A week later, I see I was wrong to despair. An armed guard arrives to convey Margaret and me to Kenninghall. My sister cries as we bid farewell to our parents and leave Staffordshire behind. I pat her back attempting to console her, but I am thrilled to be leaving and unable to sit still on my cushioned seat.

Printed in Great Britain
by Amazon